TRANSMUTE & EMPOWER

The Art of Transmuting Negative Energy into Positive Energy

Cydney Hopkins

CONTENTS

My earliest childhood memories are not one's that make me smile when I look back on them. They are traumatic, dark and confusing. I have memories of abuse, poverty, neglect and bullying.

This continued into young adult hood which caused me to develop anxiety and complex PTSD that wasn't discovered by a doctor until I was well into my early 20's.

I felt like my entire life I walked around with a dark cloud over my head and I couldn't understand why. There were so many times in my life that I should've been happy, but I just wasn't. My mind would not allow me to experience the feeling of happiness. Every moment in my life that I was supposed to feel joy were only temporary distractions from the constant doom I felt. You could never tell from the outside looking in because I became an expert at hiding it from everyone. However, whenever I had a moment alone, the darkness immediately set in.

Fast forward to 2019 when I had my daughter, Calli. That was the year that I felt true happiness for the first time in my life. Bringing a life into this world was a very spiritual experience for me and I thank God for giving me the ability to create this precious being. As beautiful as this experience was, it was also the start of my spiritual awakening, and the beginning of a journey that I was completely unprepared for to say the least.

Becoming a mother forced me to make hard but necessary changes in my life. I had someone else's childhood in my hands, and it was no longer just about me. I knew this was the beginning of breaking generational curses in real time. I began by pulling out all the darkness and trauma that was buried deep inside of me. I knew how important it was to move through the fear of this unfamiliar territory and be completely honest about the skeletons in my closet. I made a conscious decision to stop wearing my trauma like a badge of honor and begin writing a new story. I realized despite my dark past, I get to decide who I am. I made the decision to take the dirt life through at me and turn myself into a diamond.

PROLOGUE

Life's challenges and adversities can cast a dark shadow on our well-being but Cydney, a seasoned practitioner of energy transmutation, reveals the secrets to turning that shadow into a source that can empower you and help you begin again.

Allow this book to be your roadmap for transmuting negative energy into an abundant, positive force that propels you forward after dealing with what feels like constant defeat. Drawing from esoteric knowledge, modern psychology and personal experiences, Cydney Hopkins demonstrates how she was able to empower herself and navigate life's twists and turns with grace.

We will explore the impact of negativity, the benefits of transmuting energy, practical everyday exercises and empowering affirmations that will guide you on reclaiming your personal power. "Transmute and Empower" is not about avoiding challenges but about transforming them into catalysts for personal growth and self-discovery.

As you begin this journey with Cydney, you'll discover the alchemical power you have within you and unlock the ability to transmute negativity into a power that pushes you towards a more fulfilled and enriched life.

Get ready to embark on a path of self-discovery, empowerment and energetic alchemy. Your transformation begins now.

CHAPTER

One:

UNDERSTANDING NEGATIVE ENERGY

WHAT WILL YOU LEARN?

You'll learn the different types of negativity, where it comes from and how it can affect you.

The way that negative energy can have a significant impact on various aspects of your life isn't talked about enough. Negative energy and trauma can lay dormant in your body for years if not properly healed. Most people don't realize how much negativity they have suppressed over time and how its eating away at them. This is because we live in a society that does not support rest and recovery. We are programmed to conduct ourselves as robots who must dedicate most of the hours in our day to support a system that does not support us. They have designed this society in a way where we must work to eat and live. This has caused most people to put work over their mental health.

The *"powers at be"* are aware of the damage that this is causing but most of the world is not. Unfortunately, our lack of awareness doesn't stop negative energy from significantly impacting our physical and emotional wellbeing. Here are a few ways in which negative energy can affect you with or without you realizing:

HOW CAN NEGATIVE ENERGY AFFECT YOU?

1. Emotional Well-being:

Negative energy that's not properly dealt with can lead to feelings of sadness, anger and anxiety. It can create a cloud of negativity that hinders your ability to experience true joy and peace. This is one of the main ways most of us are affected by negative energy. Truthfully, most of us were not taught how to deal with negativity and as life goes on, it can begin to take its toll.

2. Relationships:

Negative energy can cause a strain on relationships with everyone around you. It can lead to unwanted conflicts and misunderstandings that can often be irreversible. Too many good people have been hurt due to the unresolved trauma of another. We can put an end to this cycle by being honest with ourselves about where we are emotionally. It's important to ask ourselves if we can take on the responsibility of a platonic or emotional relationship with another person.

3. Physical Health:

Prolonged exposure to negative energy can manifest in physical symptoms such as chronic headaches, fatigue, insomnia, weakened immune system and chronic mental illnesses. Studies have shown that negative energy can even be stored in your hips and waist, resulting in unwanted weight gain that's difficult to get rid of.

4. Mental Clarity and Focus:

Negative energy can make it difficult to think clearly and make sound decisions. It can hinder your ability to set goals, pursue passions and achieve personal growth.

5. Self-esteem and Confidence:

Negative energy can hold you back from reaching your full potential if it's not properly dealt with. It can erode your self-esteem and confidence, leading to self-doubt and feelings of worthlessness.

6. Attracting More Negativity:

Negative energy tends to attract more negativity. If you constantly dwell in negative thoughts and emotions, you may find yourself in a cycle of attracting negative experiences and people into your life. Your mind is very powerful and if you're not mindful of your thoughts, a domino effect of negativity can ruin an entire day.

Understanding the impact of negative energy is crucial because it allows you to recognize its presence and take steps to transmute it into positive energy. By doing so, you can create a more positive and fulfilling life for yourself. Too often negativity gets stored inside of your body and affects us in ways we do not realize until the damage has been done. Being mindful of your own energy and recognizing the negative patterns can help you stop them from consuming you. The cause of negativity is not always your fault but there are ways you can allow your pain to inspire you to live a better quality of life.

Make it a priority to recognize the ways you may have allowed negative energy to persist in your own life. Taking time to reflect is essential because it allows you to recognize any patterns of self-sabotage. You will be motivated to act and transmute that energy or experience into positivity. By doing this, you can break free from negative patterns and create a more fulfilling and empowered life.

CHAPTER

Two:

THE POWER OF TRANSMUTATION

> *You'll learn the concept of transmutation and how you can turn your negative experiences into empowering lessons.*

This journey requires you to look deep within at the parts you've been avoiding or may not have known were there. The moment you decide to deal with your pain and transmute your negative experiences, you are initiating yourself into an alchemical process. You are beginning a process that has the potential to change your trauma into something else.

Transmutation is not about banishing your pain from existence, it's about being brave enough to confront it head on and allow it to transform you. You cannot undo what was done to you. Those experiences will forever live inside of you and are a product of who you are today. Accepting this before you embark on this journey will help you cope with what you discover. You will find yourself expressing gratitude for your pain and begin to understand what it was trying to teach you the entire time.

Your negative experiences are just as important as your positive ones. This is where duality comes into play. We learn from physics that every action has an equal and opposite reaction. We learn from nature that sunshine is just as important as rain, as is day to night. We are much like nature in that way. Every human being has two sides to them that are a direct reflection of our negative experiences and positive experiences.

Carl Jung, a psychoanalyst, calls the version of you that was developed through negativity your shadow side. He also came up with the term shadow work, which is a concept that helps people acknowledge the parts of themselves they have suppressed. His theory was that a person could create a deeper understanding of themselves by working with their shadow side instead of running away from it.

The concept of transmutation refers to the process of transforming something from one form to another. You can find the concept of transmutation across many different masteries such as, alchemy, chemistry and spiritual development. Alchemy in a physical sense, is the transformation and altering of lead to gold. However, in spirituality, alchemy is defined as a process that liberates you into freeing the inner parts of yourself that need to be changed in order let go of what no longer serves you. Therefore, alchemy and transmutation go hand in hand.

All of us are constantly practicing transmutation without even realizing it. For example, when someone goes through a bad break up, and the pain they endured causes them to go back to school and earn their master's degree, they have practiced transmutation. They have allowed a painful experience to empower them enough to transform their life for the better. The key is the steps you take in between to reach the transformed version of yourself. In this case, it would be the long hours studying for exams, proper notes being taken in class and receiving a passing score on assignments. All these steps in between were the energy needed to earn the master's degree, which in turn transformed a hurtful experience into an empowering one.

In essence, transmutation is about recognizing the ways that your past negative experiences can be used to transform you into your highest self. When you refuse to accept defeat and are brave enough to face those dark parts of yourself head on, you can create a life that fulfills you in ways you may not have known were possible. Changing your perception of the pain you experience causes a shift in the atmosphere and creates a realm of new possibilities. Pain does not have to be the end of your story. With your permission, it can be the catalyst to your new beginning.

CHAPTER

Three:

ACKNOWLEDGE YOUR PAIN

You will learn how to validate your pain and make peace with your shadow side.

To start the alchemical process of turning negative energy into positive energy, you must acknowledge your pain. The healthiest way to do this is to face the pain or negative emotion directly and allow yourself to feel your feelings. Suppressing your feelings instead of acknowledging them is one of the worst things you could do for your mental and physical health. Ignoring what you're refusing to heal from does not make it go away. That negative energy will lay dormant inside of you until it is properly dealt with or worst case, it could manifest into a negative emotion such as rage or depression.

Acknowledging your pain also allows you to validate what you experienced and how it made you feel. What you went through was real and you're allowed to feel angry or sad about it.

You're allowed to cry, scream, or vent about the pain that you've been holding in. These actions are healthier ways to cope than minimizing your experience or forcing yourself to be strong.

Truthfully, crying is releasing the negative emotion and showing that you are in control of where the negativity goes, instead of it controlling you.

There is allot you will learn about yourself when you begin transmuting your negative experiences and emotions. Those lessons you learn are part of what makes the decision to heal so valuable. You are given the opportunity to rediscover parts of your inner child while simultaneously connecting with the highest version of yourself. When you uncover the root of your pain it helps you better understand your triggers and why you are the way you are. It also helps you come up with healthier coping mechanisms, that when used daily, creates a healthier mindset and a greater sense of self.

Deciding to transmute negative energy into positive energy allows you to truly fall in love with yourself while you're healing. This is because you learn to give yourself the grace and compassion that you may not have received before. You start to see yourself as a human worthy of love and you fight harder to give it to yourself. You're no longer weighed down by the version of you those negative experiences created. At the same time you're learning to give yourself compassion, you also discover that you have a new perception of the people around you. You begin to give grace and compassion to all beings and see everyone as their inner child.

Having a greater sense of empathy and understanding for your community helps you repair broken relationships as well as create new ones. You may even find yourself letting go of those that the transformed version of you no longer aligns with. It's okay to acknowledge that some people were only supposed to get to know the unhealed you and don't get to go into your next chapter. The relationships you keep, as well as let go of, will be a crucial part of your healing process and a true reflection of the growth you've made.

Earlier in this book I spoke on Carl Jung and his philosophy on shadow work. Shadow work has been an essential part of my own personal growth and development. It's my way of checking in with myself and seeing where I am mentally. CJ talks about how you confront your shadow side during this process, but I also see it as healing your inner child. I believe that most of your shadow side was created due to the trauma you experienced during childhood. Your shadow side is like the protector that you created to defend the child in you that didn't feel safe. Going back to your childhood can answer allot of questions about who you are today and help you get to the root of your pain. Just like your shadow side, your inner child is where your subconscious beliefs come from. These beliefs stem from how you were raised by your parents, how you were spoken to, your experience in school etc.

Below, I have provided you with three shadow work questions and space to leave your answers. You may also write down these questions in your own personal notebook and answer them there.

WHEN WAS THE FIRST MOMENT I FELT UNWORTHY?

WHAT PEOPLE, PLACES, THINGS OR EXPERIENCES TRIGGER ME THE MOST?

WHAT'S SOMETHING ABOUT MYSELF I WISH I COULD CHANGE?

As you do your inner child healing and go through this process of transmuting your negative beliefs, you will start to understand the connection between the pain you've been feeling and the negative energy that created it. For example, if your parents constantly made you feel unworthy in your youth, you may unknowingly carry this negative emotion with you into adulthood. You may develop an avoidant attachment style that causes you to run from anyone who tries to give you love because you don't feel worthy of it. In the end, running away causes you to hurt yourself more than the people you ran from because deep down inside you want love, but you're too afraid to allow yourself to receive it.

If this part of yourself isn't healed properly then you may find yourself left alone with the feeling of *"what if"*. The saying *"It's better to have loved and lost then never to love at all"* rings very true. Love is a beautiful thing that all humans are deserving of. You should allow yourself to experience it in all forms.

CHAPTER

Four:

SHIFTING PERSPECTIVES

WHAT WILL YOU LEARN?

You'll learn how to shift your perspective on your negative experiences and understand how they are an essential part of your growth.

"**What you see when you look at something depends not so much as what is there, but the perception you make when you look.**" This is a quote from Neville Goddard, a famous, English writer and speaker, that I will never forget. We are all viewing the world from a different pair of eyes. That is because none of us have the same experiences or perceive these experiences the same as the next person. When you transmute your negative emotions into more positive ones, you begin to view the world different than you did before. You begin to feel less like a victim and more like a victor. This newfound perception you've created through healing can give you a better quality of life overall. This is because our thoughts and feelings create our reality. When you are holding onto negative energy and emotions, the way you perceive the world is also negative.

Releasing negative energy and transmuting it into positive energy allows for the world around you to become more positive. This does not mean you will not run into unfortunate events; it just means that the way you perceive these events will be different because you are experiencing them from a more positive emotional state. For example, if someone cuts you off in traffic while you're in a good mood, you are more likely to laugh it off. However, if you are in a bad mood, you may chase the other driver down putting them and yourself in danger. Same event, different reactions due to different perspectives, leading to different outcomes.

Part of the human experience is acknowledging that we are emotional creatures. Still, it does not mean we have to be controlled by our emotions all the time. Allowing your emotions to control you instead of controlling them can put you in detrimental situations. This is why emotional intelligence is so important and should be practiced often. Emotional intelligence isn't the lack of a response, it's how you respond that matters. To control your emotions and create fewer negative experiences, you must learn how to reframe them. Here are some techniques you can practice helping you better control your negative emotions and feelings:

1. **Cognitive Restructuring:**

   This is a technique that involves identifying negative and irrational thoughts and challenging them. It gives you the opportunity to question the validity of these negative beliefs so you can replace them with more positive alternatives. For instance, if a negative intrusive thought comes to you and says, *"Nobody will ever love me."* You can decide in that moment that you do not agree with that thought. Take a moment to send the thought on its way and replace it with a more positive belief such as, *"I am someone worthy of being loved."* Not only is this cognitive restructuring, it's also a form of transmutation.

2. **Mindfulness and Acceptance:**

   The most important part of this healing process is to observe whatever comes up without judgement.

Practice being mindful of each thought that comes to mind and listen considerately like you would to a child that's telling a story. Your negative thoughts are just as normal as your positive thoughts and equally as important. Your negative thoughts are there to teach you something about your shadow side. Trying to suppress them instead of listening to what that part of you has to say is the same a neglecting the inner child in you looking to be heard. Accepting that the part of you that feels negative emotions is real can help reduce resistance and facilitate emotional processing and healing.

3. Express Gratitude:

One of my favorite ways to transmute negative energy and empower myself through dark times, is by simply expressing gratitude. Making gratitude apart of your everyday life will cause a major shift in your mental state and overall wellbeing. When you are going through a difficult time it makes it harder to remember everything that you should be thankful for. The world as you know it begins to fade to the background because you're trapped in your head focusing on everything negative. Although this is very common, this is a crucial time to remember to express gratitude for even the little things. Doing this is transmuting negative feelings and calling in more positive experiences.

The universe recognizes and blesses those who are grateful for what they already have, with more. This is because people who are vibrating in a state of gratitude are in alignment with abundance. They are never lacking anything because they feel they have everything they need.

AFFIRMATIONS

"I INVITE GRATITUDE INTO MY HEART"

*"I AM DEEPLY GRATEFUL FOR ALL
THAT I AM BLESSED WITH."*

*"I AM GRATEFUL FOR EVERYTHING I HAVE
WHILE BEING OPEN AND RECEPTIVE TO
MORE."*

*"EVERY CELL IN MY BODY VIBRATES WITH
GRATITUDE."*

*"THANK YOU FOR THE BLESSINGS THIS DAY
BRINGS."*

4. **Visualization:**

The mind can be a very powerful tool if used correctly. Anything you create in a thought form is capable of manifesting into a physical form. This is because your thoughts are electric, and your feelings are magnetic.

When we produce a thought, it's done by our brain releasing chemicals called neurotransmitters. Our neurotransmitters generate electrical signals to our neurons causing the electrical signals to circulate out to more neurons. This leads to the formation of a thought. Each thought we make generates a unique energetic frequency emitting electromagnetic waves into the atmosphere.

When you pair the electricity that a thought produces with the magnetism of your feelings, you have the power to bring whatever you visualize into your reality.

Knowing this is why we must be careful with how we speak to ourselves and others. Even more so we should be mindful of how we feel. Make it a point to surround yourself with people, places and things that make you feel good so you can release that goodness back into the world.

5. **Journaling:**

There's something so healing about sitting down with a pen and paper and letting your thoughts flow onto the page. Observe whatever comes up without judgement and allow your thoughts to guide you to write out how you're feeling. It doesn't matter how dark or negative it is; it's being brought to your attention for a reason. This is a form of releasing and could possibly help you transmute whatever negativity is lingering in your mind. I suggest you keep a journal specifically for this technique because you will be able to look back on how much you have grown.

6. Professional Therapy:

Consider seeking therapy or counseling to work through deeper emotional issues and develop personalized strategies for reframing negative emotions. A trained therapist can provide you with the guidance and support you need, and tools tailored to your specific circumstances.

Reframing negative experiences and emotions is a skill that takes practice and persistence. The most important thing to remember is not to judge yourself through this process and be patient with yourself through each step. There is no quick fix to reprogramming your mind and you shouldn't expect perfection. However, if you incorporate these techniques into your daily life, you can develop a more resilient, positive and empowered mindset, enabling you to navigate life's challenges with ease.

CHAPTER
Five:
CULTIVATING POSITIVE ENERGY

You'll learn the different ways to cultivate positive energy in order to raise your frequency.

When you are doing alchemy, how you treat your mind and body is important. You are changing one form of energy to another form which can cause physical change to your body. If you aren't the type of person that prioritizes self-care, there's no better time to start then right now. Doing self-care will help you through this alchemical process and help produce more positive energy.

Self-care isn't just all bubble baths and candles. Self-care is being kind to your overall being. Nurturing and caring for yourself the way you would a child. Speak kindly to yourself, put good things in your body and don't surround yourself with people who don't align with who you are.

How much care you give to yourself is a direct reflection of how much you love yourself. Love of self means that you prioritize your peace above all else. Someone who moves this way is happier than someone who puts themselves last. The state of happiness you develop from doing self-care causes you to raise your vibration and make transmuting negative energy allot easier.

Here are some practical tips to help you incorporate more positive energy into your life:

1. Meditation:

Meditation is a practice that has changed my life. As someone who has had my struggles with anxiety, I find that doing daily mindfulness meditations has almost dissipated my anxious thoughts. Practicing mindfulness meditations regularly will bring you a sense of peace and calm that is necessary when trying to cultivate positive energy. This state of calm will give you a "high off life" feeling that has you vibrating at a higher frequency. Mediation can also help you become more aware of your own thoughts, emotions and sensations. This is important when practicing the art of transmutation because you will know exactly where the energy is coming from. Knowing thy self will allow you to respond to life's challenges with greater clarity and poise.

2. Positive Affirmations:

Have you ever heard the phrase words are spells? This statement couldn't be truer, which is why it's important to be mindful of what you speak out into the universe. You are sending out a signal to the universe and it will respond accordingly. To take it a step further, I will add that your belief in what you are saying is the magic behind the spell you are casting over your life. Choose every word carefully. Once I grasped this concept I started incorporating positive affirmations into my everyday life. Saying affirmations is another form of transmutation because you are challenging and replacing negative self-talk. Repeat empowering and uplifting statements to yourself regularly if you want to promote a positive self-image and mindset.

AFFIRMATIONS

"I am abundant in all areas of my life."

"I am worthy of love in all forms."

*"I am grateful for everything I have while being
open and receptive to more."*

"I love and appreciate myself for who I am."

"I choose authenticity over perfection."

3. Physical Activity:

Physical activity releases endorphins, which are "happy chemicals" that can help reduce stress and anxiety. Exercise can also help move negative energy around and is a great way to transmute energy if you are having a bad day. However, as I got older I began to understand that exercise and physical activity is not a one size fits all type of thing. You must find one that works for you and that your body can keep up with, so you won't quit before you see results. Yoga, Pilates, walking, jogging, swimming, tennis, dancing and lifting weights are a few of the many options you have when it comes to picking a physical activity. Pick one or more that suits your lifestyle so you can keep your body in shape, decrease stress and create a happier overall wellbeing.

4. Healthy Diet:

It's important to maintain a balanced and nutritious diet, rich in fruits, vegetables, whole grains, lean proteins and healthy fats. Having the right diet can support your physical and mental well-being, providing you with the energy and strength needed to maintain a positive outlook on life.

5. Breath Work:

There are a variety of breathing techniques and exercises designed to improve your mental and spiritual well-being by enhancing the connection you have between the mind and body. Breathwork is a practice that has been used for thousands of years in various cultures and traditions to promote relaxation, reduce stress and facilitate self-awareness and healing.

Below I have provided a list of key aspects of breath work and different exercises that you can begin incorporating regularly:

- **Conscious Breathing:** Breath-work puts an emphasis on intentional breathing where you focus on the depth of your breath. This involves paying attention to the rhythm, pace and pattern of your breathing. Slowing down and deepening your breath is known to induce a sense of relaxation and calm.

- **Body Awareness:** Breath work involves developing an awareness of how your body is communicating to you. It allows you to pay attention to your body's sensations, feelings and responses as you take each breath. The awareness you develop through your breath work can help you identify areas of stress or imbalance and help you release any physical and emotional tension.

- **Presence:** Breath work supports mindfulness and presence by anchoring your attention to the present moment through each breath. This helps you quiet the mind, reduce intrusive thoughts, and cultivate a sense of inner stillness.

TYPES OF BREATH WORK:

- **Wim Hof Method:** The Wim Hof Method is a unique breath work technique developed by Dutch athlete Wim Hof. His method combines specific breathing patterns, cold exposure and mindset training. This has been shown to help people with depression, mood swings, anxiety and mental clarity. The goal of this breath work exercise is to help you develop control over your nervous system, immune system and cardiovascular system to be stronger and happier.

- **Box Breathing:** Box breathing, also known as square breathing, is a simple and effective breath work technique that involves inhaling deeply, holding the breath, exhaling, and holding the breath again in equal counts. This practice can help reduce stress, improve your focus and concentration, and bring you a sense of balance.

- **Transformational Breath work:** Transformational breath work brings a more therapeutic approach to breath work that combines conscious breathing with sound, movement, and emotional release techniques to enable healing. It's been known to cause a transformation physically, emotionally, and spiritually.

Breath work can reduce stress, improve mental focus and enhance your overall being. It's a powerful and versatile practice that offers a wide range of benefits for the mind, body, and soul. Whether you're seeking stress relief, improved mental clarity or emotional healing, incorporating breathwork into your daily routine can be a valuable tool for providing you with greater balance and harmony in your life.

6. Time with Mother Nature:

Putting away electronics and spending time outdoors helps recharge and rejuvenate your being. When you connect with nature on the regular it allows you to ground your energy and find clarity in the peace in quiet. Whether it's a walk in the park, hiking in the mountains, sitting by a lake with your toes in the grass or submerging your body in the ocean, connecting with nature can help foster a sense of awe and gratitude.

7. Limit Exposure to Negativity:

These days it's common for us to get caught up in technology and forget to live in the real world. It's important to be mindful of your media consumption and limit exposure to negative news. Allot of the media that's pushed out onto the masses is designed to cause fear in the collective. Fear lowers your vibration and keeps you from being able to manifest properly and connect with the divine. Toxic relationships and environments are also things that can potentially drain your energy. If you can cut off a toxic relationship or leave a toxic environment, then its important you do so to create the peaceful life you deserve. Make it your mission to surround yourself with positive influences, uplifting content and a supportive community who inspires and encourage you.

By incorporating these practices into your daily life, you can create a life filled with joy and fulfillment. Remember that creating positivity is an ongoing journey and it's okay to start small and gradually build upon these practices over time. No matter what give yourself grace and patience and be proud of your decision to take this step.

CHAPTER

Six:

THE ALCHEMY OF TRANSMUTATION

You'll learn the alchemical process of transmuting negative energy into positive energy.

Alchemist believed that the elixir of life could be derived from the philosopher's stone. In western alchemy, the philosophers stone is an object capable of turning metal into gold bringing health and longevity. This is the similar alchemical process that you will undergo as you begin transmuting negative energy into positive energy. If you take the negative energy and experiences life gave you and begin to view them from a higher perspective, you will be given *"eternal life."* This eternal life comes from your ability to alchemize any energy that's thrown at you. Negative energy will no longer be able to destroy you because you know what to do with it, thus you never *die*, you only transition.

KEY PRINCIPLES OF ALCHEMY:

1. The Three Principles:

Alchemy traditionally operates on the principles of Sulphur, Mercury, and Salt. They represent these three essential phases of transformation: the Soul (Sulphur), the Spirit (Mercury), and the Body (Salt). These principles symbolize the harmonization of the spiritual, mental, and physical aspects of the individual.

2. The Great Work:

The "Great Work" or *"Magnum Opus"* is the goal of alchemy. This is the process of achieving spiritual enlightenment, self-realization and wholeness through the transformation and purification of the self. It involves:

- **Calcination**: The first stage of the alchemical process involves burning and purifying yourself, letting go of ego, illusions, and attachments.

- **Dissolution**: The second stage involves dissolving and releasing emotional and psychological blockages, traumas, and negative patterns.

- **Separation**: The third stage involves separating and discerning the essential from the non-essential. You will begin distinguishing your authentic self from your ego and integrating the shadow aspects of who you are.

- **Conjunction**: The fourth stage involves balancing the masculine and feminine energies, thus achieving inner harmony and wholeness.

- **Fermentation**: The fifth stage is about nurturing the inner transformation. This is where you allow the new self to mature and evolve.

- **Distillation**: The sixth stage involves refining and purifying yourself, extracting the essence of your experiences, insights, and wisdom.

- **Coagulation**: The final stage is about grounding yourself in the transformation you've undergone. This is the point where you begin embodying your higher self and manifesting your true potential and purpose in the world.

THE ALCHEMY OF TRANSMUTATION:

Alchemy encourages you to elevate your consciousness, expand your awareness and awaken to higher states of being, or your *highest self*. It involves integrating and harmonizing the various aspects of the mind, body, emotions, and spirit. This will help you achieve inner balance and alignment with your true purpose.

Transmutation is a journey of soul alchemy where you learn to transform your challenges, struggles and negative experiences into opportunities for growth, learning and empowerment. It involves acknowledging and embracing what's hiding in your shadows. Once you recognize your shadow side, including your fears and insecurities, you'll begin to cultivate more positive qualities. This is because the healing process you go through causes you to transmute negativity into love, compassion, courage and resilience.

Your mind begins to heal as you transmute your negative experiences. You begin to see the brighter side of things due to the newfound love and compassion you have for yourself and your journey. This causes you to align with your highest self. Your higher self is where your true core values and spiritual purpose lies. It is the true essence that leads you down the path towards a meaningful life.

I came up with my own three-step process on the art of transmutation and how to alchemize negative energy into positive energy. These three steps are called: *Fall*, *Rise*, and *Land*. The **Fall** is the negative experience or emotion. The **Rise** is the steps you take to pull yourself out of the negative experience. The **Land** is you arriving successfully in the new, positive state of being.

You are only able to arrive in the new positive experience when you take the proper steps to pull yourself out of the negative one.

There are three things you must keep in mind to safely maneuver through this practice: **1.** Each step is necessary and must be done in order. **2.** There is no time limit to when you complete this process. It could take hours, days, weeks, months or even years. The choice is completely up to you. **3.** Each time you go through this alchemical process you may fall harder than you did before, but you will always rise higher than you did before.

Earlier in this book I mentioned how we are constantly transmuting energy without even realizing it. However, there is something powerful about transmuting energy with intention. Below I have provided space for you to write out how you intend to transmute your negative experience or emotion into a more positive, favorable outcome. This could be changing from broke to rich, alcoholic to sober, overweight to dream body or living with your parents to being a homeowner, to name a few. Utilize the space provided to you below but also copy this concept into your own personal notebook whenever you need it.

THE FALL: WHAT NEGATIVE ENERGY, EXPERIENCE OR EMOTION ARE YOU TRYING TO TRANSMUTE AND OVERCOME?

THE RISE: WHAT STEPS WILL YOU TAKE TO OVERCOME THIS NEGATIVE ENERGY, EXPERIENCE OR EMOTION?

THE LAND: WHAT NEW POSITIVE EXPERIENCE OR OUTCOME DO YOU WANT TO LAND ON?

CHAPTER
Seven:
EMBRACING YOUR PERSONAL POWER

WHAT WILL YOU LEARN?

You'll learn how to embrace the personal power you created from your negative experiences.

Transmutation and personal power are interconnected concepts that reflect the transformative potential within you to harness your experiences for personal growth. As we discussed earlier, it refers to the process of changing something from one form or state into another. In the case of personal development and spirituality, transmutation involves transforming negative energies, emotions, beliefs, and experiences into positive and empowering ones. Through this process you will learn to acknowledge and accept your feelings and emotions, including the negative ones, as valuable parts of your journey.

Personal power refers to the strength that you possess to take charge of your life and create the life you desire. It's about developing a deep understanding of yourself, including your strengths, weaknesses, beliefs and fears. Through this empowering process, you will be able to cultivate the confidence you need to assert yourself and take aligned action. Being empowered is also about taking responsibility for you own actions and using what you learned to grow and evolve.

By learning to transmute negative energy, you will be able to reclaim your power and turn obstacles into steppingstones towards personal and spiritual evolution. You will be become a master of self while you learn to navigate and transform your internal landscape of emotions and beliefs. This process of self-transformation promotes personal growth, self-empowerment, and the development of your own personal power. You will be able to align more closely with your authentic self and higher purpose. This alignment will strengthen your sense of self, enhance your self-confidence and inspire you to live a life that is more meaningful and fulfilling.

Transmutation and personal power are complementary aspects of personal development and spiritual growth. Transmutation provides the tools you need for transforming challenges into opportunities for growth, while personal power reflects the inner strength and autonomy that enables you to create a life that is aligned with your authentic self. By embracing the process of transmutation and cultivating personal power, you could unlock your full potential and create a life filled with purpose.

CONCLUSION

In this book we talked about the different types of negative energy and how it can affect your wellbeing and quality of life. Education on this topic is important because it helps you get to the root of why you are the way you are and why you react the way you do. Most of us were not taught how to properly deal with our emotions and that's something society should change. We do not have to fall victim to our triggers, we only need to understand them and allow our understanding to help us transmute the energy into something more empowering. You have a right to walk around in a body that you feel safe in. As someone who used to walk around feeling like I was surrounded by darkness every second of the day, I can confidently say I am genuinely happy. Up until age 20 I thought I was cursed, but even through the impeding gloom, something inside me refused to die. It wasn't until I realized that I had the power to write a new story for myself and act on it, that life begin to get better. I now understand why I couldn't accept defeat. Defeat was where my story began but it's not where it ends.

You are not your trauma and you do not have to carry the weight of every negative experience you've ever had on your shoulders. You can take back control of your life. Instead of allowing the pain to weigh you down, let it to raise you up. Allow the old you to die and hold a service in their honor. Do not be ashamed of past versions of yourself, instead express gratitude for each one. Without them, there would be no you. Every negative experience and emotion you experienced was essential so you could arrive at this point in time. This is the moment you get to rise to the top, on the back of the trauma that thought it had won; accompanied by the skeletons that got tired of hiding.